W9-CKL-377
DISCARD

American Holidays / Celebraciones en los Estados Unidos

MARTIN LUTHER KING JR. DAY
NATALICIO DE MARTIN LUTHER KING JR.

Connor Dayton Traducción al español: Eduardo Alamán

PowerKiDS press
New York

Published in 2012 by The Rosen Publishing Group, Inc.
29 East 21st Street, New York, NY 10010

First Edition

Editor: Jennifer Way
Book Design: Julio Gil

Traducción al español: Eduardo Alamán

Photo Credits: Cover, p. 19 Jewel Samad/AFP/Getty Images; p. 5 Susan Stocker/South Florida Sun Sentinel/MCT via Getty Images; pp. 7, 17 Rolls Press/Popperfoto/Getty Images; pp. 9, 24 (bottom) Francis Miller/Time & Life Pictures/Getty Images; p. 11 Don Cravens/Time & Life Pictures/Getty Images; pp. 13, 24 (top left) William Lovelace/Express/Getty Images; pp. 14–15 Hulton Archive/Getty Images; pp. 21, 24 (top right) Jim West/age fotostock; p. 23 Alex Wong/Getty Images.

Library of Congress Cataloging-in-Publication Data

Dayton, Connor.
[Martin Luther King Jr. Day. Spanish & English]
Martin Luther King Jr. Day = Natalicio de Martin Luther King Jr. / by Connor Dayton. — 1st ed.
p. cm. — (American holidays = Celebraciones en los Estados Unidos)
Includes index.
ISBN 978-1-4488-6710-3 (library binding)
1. Martin Luther King, Jr., Day—Juvenile literature. 2. King, Martin Luther, Jr., 1929–1968—Juvenile literature. I. Title. II. Title: Natalicio de Martin Luther King Jr.
E185.97.K5D3618 2012
394.261—dc23

2011024115

Web Sites: Due to the changing nature of Internet links, PowerKids Press has developed an online list of Web sites related to the subject of this book. This site is updated regularly. Please use this link to access the list:
www.powerkidslinks.com/amh/king/

Manufactured in the United States of America

CPSIA Compliance Information: Batch #WW12PK: For Further Information contact Rosen Publishing, New York, New York at 1-800-237-9932

Contents

Contenido

Martin Luther King Jr. Day is the third Monday in January. It honors a great American leader.

El Natalicio de Martin Luther King Jr. se celebra el tercer lunes de enero. Honra a un gran líder de los Estados Unidos.

I Am
A
Promise!
I Am
A
Promis

Martin Luther King Jr. was born on January 15, 1929. He was born in Atlanta, Georgia.

Martin Luther King Jr. nació el 15 de enero de 1929, en Atlanta, Georgia.

King spoke out against laws that were unfair to African Americans. He helped change these laws.

King se manifestó contra las leyes que no eran justas para los afroamericanos. King ayudó a cambiar esas leyes.

The work to change these unfair laws is called the civil rights movement.

El movimiento que ayudó a cambiar estas leyes se conoce como el movimiento de los derechos civiles.

King wanted people to work for civil rights peacefully.

King deseaba que la gente obtuviera estos derechos de manera pacífica.

King was known for leading **marches**. His biggest march was the March on Washington in 1963.

King fue famoso por sus **manifestaciones**. Su marcha más grande fue en marzo de 1963, en Washington.

UAW

King was known for his **speeches**, too. His best-known speech is his "I have a dream" speech.

Además, King es famoso por sus **discursos**. Su discurso más famoso es el llamado "Yo tengo un sueño".

Martin Luther King Jr. Day honors King. It honors civil rights, too.

El Natalicio de Martin Luther King Jr. honra a King y al movimiento de los derechos civiles.

NATIONAL
PARK
SERVICE

People spend the holiday as a day of **service**. This means doing things to help your community.

Las personas celebran este día haciendo **servicios**. Esto significa que trabajan para ayudar a la comunidad.

Ω
Ψ
Φ

How do you celebrate Martin Luther King Jr. Day?

¿Cómo celebras el Natalicio de Martin Luther King Jr.?